BE STRONG!

HOW TO LIVE VICTORIOUSLY IN DIFFICULT CIRCUMSTANCES

BE STRONG!

How to Live Victoriously in Difficult Circumstances

MIRANDA BURNETTE

Keys to Success Publishing
Atlanta, GA

KEYS TO SUCCESS PUBLISHING

Be Strong: How to Live Victoriously in Difficult Circumstances

ISBN: 978-0-9998938-9-0

P. O. Box 314
Clarkdale, GA 30111

www.mirandaburnetteministries.org

Keys to Success Publishing
Atlanta, GA 30127

Cover Design by Jackie Moore

DEDICATION

I dedicate this book, Be Strong, to my best friend and sister in the Lord, Gleta Green, one of the most spiritually strong people I know. Gleta, STAY STRONG in the Lord and in HIS MIGHTY POWER as you fight life's battles and WIN. You are more than a conqueror!

TABLE OF CONTENTS

Dedication v

Introduction ix

CHAPTER 1: Be Strong... 1

CHAPTER 2: The Belt of Truth.................................. 11

CHAPTER 3: The Breastplate of Righteousness 17

CHAPTER 4: The Shoes of the Gospel of Peace.......... 25

CHAPTER 5: The Shield of Faith 37

CHAPTER 6: The Helmet of Salvation........................ 47

CHAPTER 7: The Sword of the Spirit......................... 55

CHAPTER 8: A Challenge to Stand Firm 63

INTRODUCTION

Do you have battles in your life you have to fight? We all fight battles in life! Everyone is fighting some kind of battle. We all have battles in some form or another. Whether it is a family situation, a relationship struggle, a financial issue, a long-standing problem that seems to never go away, we all fight battles!

"Everyone you meet is fighting a battle you know nothing about. Be kind. Always. "

_Brad Meltzer

The question is this: Are you fighting those battles in your own strength or relying on the supernatural power of God? When you battle with the adversity in life with God on your side, you can make it and win.

No matter how big your opponent, no matter how fierce your enemy looks, no matter how critical or hopeless your sickness appears to be, with God, you can make.

There is a war going on. We are in a war! The battle is raging! To win this war, we have to be strong and equipped for the fight. To be strong, we have to put on our armor, the whole armor of God! Not just part of the armor, we need the full armor God has already prepared for us to use.

This is spiritual armor because the battle that is going on is in the spiritual realm. This is a spiritual battle that we can't see. We are in a spiritual war. But, God has equipped us with six powerful, very effective weapons and armor, with which to fight and come out victoriously. Of which, if we use, we won't lose. We won't lose when we put on this very mighty, dynamic armor of God.

All of us, at various times in our lives, will face battles. The spiritual battles that we fight are against an unseen enemy. So how do you fight this invisible enemy and win every time? As you read the following chapters in *Be Strong: How to Live Victoriously in Difficult Circumstances,* you will find out.

There are many types of unseen enemies we have to fight in life each day and others that we have to fight from time to time, such as COVID-19, racism, politics, the economy, and many others, including our personal issues.

It is hard enough to have to fight an enemy *you can* see, but when you have to fight an enemy you *can't see,* an unseen enemy, that is tough! But with God, we can conquer any unseen enemy and win the battles we face in life.

God has already equipped us for the battles of life. So let's put on our armor and get ready for the fight.

You cannot stand up to and fight spiritual enemies through physical strength and physical means. To overcome spiritual enemies, one must exercise spiritual means.

The armor God has given to us is invisible. So how do we put on something we can't see? The armor is also spiritual. Its purpose is to protect us in this spiritual war. We put on this invisible, spiritual armor by faith.

When the enemy tries to get you to worry, give up on your dreams, make wrong choices, or think negative thoughts about yourself or other people, you can get dressed for battle by putting on God's full armor and standing strong. So, let's get dressed. It is time to put on the armor of God and prepare to win life's battle.

If we focus our attention on the things we *can see,* such as people, circumstances, problems, national issues, boss issues, racial division, and other difficulties, we will forget about the real spiritual enemy we *can't see.*

We have an enemy behind the scene of all of this mess that is going on in the world right now. The unseen enemy comes to kill, steal, and destroy. But Jesus came so that we might have life and have it more abundantly and to the full *(John 10:10).*

A familiar battle strategy, and one of the first things in the battles we have to fight in life is, "You have got to know your enemy." Satan is the source of all hatred, strife, turmoil, misery, suffering, and the battles we fight. Satan is the source of all problems.

We often lose the battle because we don't know, nor do we understand the enemy. We have to realize that our battle is not with people or circumstances.

Ephesians 6:12 tells us that we wrestle not with flesh and blood.

Satan works through circumstances and people. Our part is to resist the devil, not necessarily the circumstances or the people giving us trouble.

When Satan works through people and circumstances, what is he trying to accomplish in our lives? The following are just a few of the things he is trying to do to us:

> ➤ He wants to steal our joy because the joy of the Lord is our strength.

> ➤ He wants to steal our peace because peace is power.

> ➤ He wants us to disobey God.

> ➤ He wants to cause division, because there is power in unity, and God commands His blessing upon unity.

➢ He wants to create strife in our lives. With God's strength, we can love our enemies.

➢ He wants us to complain and speak death over our situations.

➢ He wants us to worry and become confused. With God's help, we can remain calm during a crisis in life.

➢ He wants us to doubt and not believe God's Word.

➢ He wants us to fear, which is the opposite of faith.

➢ He wants us to be hopeless and give up.

The full armor of God is described in Ephesians 6:10-18. The full armor includes the following pieces: the belt of truth, the breastplate of righteousness, the shoes of the gospel of peace, the shield of faith, the helmet of salvation, and the sword of the Spirit.

There are a total of six pieces of armor. In the following chapters of this book, we will explore each piece of armor in depth. You will discover what each part is and how to use each one in your life to win the battles you face and come out victoriously.

CHAPTER 1

BE STRONG!

Finally, be strong in the Lord and in his mighty power.

__ Ephesians 6:10 (NIV)

To be strong and armored to fight the battles we encounter in life and win; we must be spiritually fit. Do you have strength for the battle? To fulfill our calling, reach our full God-given potential, realize our dreams, and achieve our goals, it is imperative, it is vitally important for each of us to be strong in the Lord and in His mighty power.

How do we become and stay strong? We become and stay strong by being equipped for the battles we are going to face in life. We equip ourselves by spending time with God and developing an intimate relationship with Him on a daily basis.

We spend time with God by reading, studying, meditating, confessing, and declaring His Word. We spend time with God by praying, praising, and worshipping Him. We spend time with God by practicing His presence, talking to Him throughout the day, and acknowledging Him in all things. We spend time with God by going to church, fellowshipping with other believers, and encouraging one another in the Word of God.

We have to have a *'winner's attitude'* and lean and depend on God to win the battles in our lives. He won't let us down! God wants you to fulfill your potential and do His will as much as or more than you do. So be strong in God's mighty power so you will be able to stand firm when obstacles come your way that try to stop you from fulfilling your God-given potential.

It is only as you work out spiritual that you will become strong in the Lord and in the power of His might. If we are going to defeat and overcome the opposition in this spiritual war, we must always be in training for the battle to become strong soldiers. So exercise your spiritual muscles and stay strong!

GROWING STRONGER AND STRONGER!

The only way to become stronger and stronger when we do physical exercise is to workout consistently by exercising, lifting weights, and pushing ourselves, even when it gets hard. When you work out physically, you become stronger in direct proportion to the time, energy, and effort you invest in your workout routine.

This is also true if you desire to become a stronger Christian. You will only become a stronger Christian in direct proportion to the time, energy, and effort you invest in practicing the Christian disciplines, such as Bible study, praying, praising God, and so forth. Becoming strong in the Lord and in the power of His might won't happen automatically.

The verse of scripture above, *Ephesians 6:10,* begins by informing us to be strong in the Lord and in the power of His might. But how do we accomplish this? The next verse, *Ephesians 6:11,* instructs us to put on the whole armor of God.

Putting on the whole armor and using the spiritual weapons God has provided for us, is God's step-by-step Battle Plan for winning every battle we fight. This will empower us to BE STRONG in the Lord and in the power of His might, as we let God fight our battles!

LET GOD FIGHT YOUR BATTLES!

Exodus 13:14 (ESV) says, The Lord will fight for you, and you have only to be silent.

Very often, we try to fight our own battles instead of letting God fight our battles. I am not saying that we should do nothing, but we should do only what God leads us to do. We need to do it when He tells us to do it and how he tells us to do it.

Otherwise, we should stand back and get out of God's way. We must let Him fight our battles--his way, in His timing, and how He chooses to fight them. God knows how to handle our battles a whole lot better than we do.

"For My thoughts are not your thoughts, and My ways are not your ways," says the Lord. "For as the heavens are higher than the earth, so are My ways higher than your ways, and My thoughts than your thoughts."

__Isaiah 55:8-9 (NLV)

Isaiah 55:8-9 (NLV) lets us know that God's ways are not our ways, and his ways are higher than our ways. So we need to get out of God's way. Let God be God!

We often hinder God's help because we are trying to do something in our own human strength that only God can do. We need to take our hands off of it. We don't need to help God. God doesn't need our help. We don't need to do God's job. Let God do His job. Our job is to believe God.

You may have a situation on your job that did not go the way you hoped it would go. So you get in there and begin to try to straighten it out. You did not pray about it first. During all that time, the Lord is speaking to your heart, telling you to leave it alone and be quiet.

After you have acted in your own way, spoken things you shouldn't have, ignored the Holy Spirit's prompting, and have been disobedient to God, you feel awful. You regret it because now the situation is much worse than before you got so deeply involved trying to solve it yourself.

We need to learn how to lean and depend on God and trust Him with all of our heart. Situations will work out so much better for us, and we won't wind up in so many difficult circumstances, not realizing how we got ourselves into so much trouble. We will save ourselves a lot of heartache and pain. God's ways work if we will work them. That means if we give God a chance to move on our behalf and stay out of his way, things will work out for us. We need to let it go and let God. We need to cast our cares upon Him.

He is waiting to help us if we would only give Him a chance. Give God a chance to solve your problems. He won't let you down.

Deuteronomy 20:4 (ESV) says, "For the Lord your God is he who goes with you to fight for you against your enemies, to give you the victory."

We have to get out of God's way. God sees the big picture, and He knows all of the facts. He knows the people involved better than we do, and He has control of their hearts. God is the only one who can change them or change their minds.

We can't change people, but God can. He can also maneuver and orchestrate situations in a way that we could only imagine. We need to get out of God's way and let him fight our battles. His ways are higher than our ways.

He may have a more excellent plan than what we can see with the natural eye. He may have a supernatural plan in mind. God's plan is so much greater than ours because it is a supernatural plan. Also, as the verse above states, God's thoughts are not our thoughts. God doesn't think as we think. His ways are so much higher than our ways. That is why we should look to God.

He is THE way maker. He can make a way out of no way. There is no problem too hard for God to solve. So get out of God's way and let him fight your battles today, and you will walk out in victory!

STAND STRONG AS A SOLDIER OF GOD

We are soldiers in God's army. As a soldier of God, we are armed and dangerous! Do you ever feel as though you are battling in a war each day? You should take time to make sure your armor can stand up to the fight.

Ephesians 6:11-18 (NIV)

Put on the full armor of God, so that you can take your stand against the devil's schemes.

For our struggle is not against flesh and blood, but against the rulers, against the authorities, against the powers of this dark world and against the spiritual forces of evil in the heavenly realms.

Therefore, put on the full armor of God, so that when the day of evil comes, you may be able to stand your ground, and after you have done everything, to stand.

Stand firm then, with the belt of truth buckled around your waist, with the breastplate of righteousness in place,

and with your feet fitted with the readiness that comes from the gospel of peace.

In addition to all this, take up the shield of faith, with which you can extinguish all the flaming arrows of the evil one.

Take the helmet of salvation and the sword of the Spirit, which is the word of God.

And pray in the Spirit on all occasions with all kinds of prayers and request. With this in mind, be alert and always keep on praying for all the Lord's people.

The ancient church in Ephesus was a new diversified and growing church of new Believers. Paul wrote them this letter to help them develop into strong Christians.

Paul wanted to help them fulfill the purpose and calling God had given to them. He reminded them, as this letter does for you and me, to put on all of God's armor so that we will be able to stand firm against all the devil's strategies and schemes when he comes against us. Paul told the *Ephesians,* and he is also telling us how we can win our battles.

When a Roman soldier was close to the front on the battlefield, he usually wore his armor day and night. He did not want to be found defenseless during a surprise attack by the enemy.

We must realize that, as long as we are in this world, we are on enemy territory. We are constantly at the front. We cannot afford to become negligent and lay down our armor. We must be determined to keep our armor on.

A soldier on the battlefield can't afford to let their guard down, because they could come under attack at any moment. We must never let our guard down. We must always be prepared for an enemy's attack. We must always wear the full armor of God.

Matthew 26:41 (NIV) says, "Watch and pray so that you will not fall into temptation. The Spirit is willing, but the flesh is weak."

2 Timothy 2:4 (NIV) says, "No one serving as a soldier gets entangled in civilian affairs, but rather tries to please his commanding officer."

Soldiers don't get tied up in the affairs of civilian life. Our spiritual war is not always easy. At times, it is intense and fearsome. That is the nature of combat.

Remember the promises given to us in this passage. *Verse 11* says, "If we put on the full armor of God, we will be able to stand firm against the schemes of the devil."

Verse 13 says, "If we take up the full armor of God, we will be able to resist in the evil day, and having done everything to stand firm." What is *the evil day?*

The evil day is any day that we are tempted, that we are distressed, that we go through or experience persecution or trials. By that definition, every day is an *evil day.* But we can, by wearing and using God's armor and weapons, stand victoriously!

God has given us some very powerful armor to use to defeat our enemy. This armor consists of five defensive pieces and one offensive piece. The defensive parts are to protect us from our enemy. The offensive part, the sword of the Spirit, which is the Word of God, is used to attack the enemy.

The defensive pieces are the belt of Truth, the breastplate of righteousness, the shoes of the gospel of peace, the shield of faith, and the helmet of salvation. We will discuss each piece of this armor in the following chapters by learning what they are and how to use each piece.

CHAPTER 2

THE BELT OF TRUTH

Stand firm then, with the belt of truth buckled around your waist,

__Ephesians 6:14 (NIV)

The Belt of Truth would have been the first piece of protective equipment the soldier put on when he was preparing for battle. The soldier's belt gave him a place to hang his sword. The belt equipped the soldier for battle.

To be *"fitted with the belt"* meant he was ready to face action. The belt was used to tie up the soldier's garments or to tuck in his loose tunic so it would not get in the way while the soldier was marching or fighting in a battle.

When you make certain you are a person of Truth, you can be prepared in every circumstance. You can do this by being a person with good character and integrity and walking in God's love.

The Roman soldier wore a belt that was made of metal with thick heavy leather. The belt had a protective piece that hung down in the front. The soldier's belt held all of the other sections of his armor together.

Truth is also the belt that holds the Believer's armor together. Truth can be found in God's Word. We must know this Truth to protect ourselves from the *"father of lies."*

The belt secured the different parts of armor, which allowed the soldier to move around freely. Truth also ensures us and gives us freedom in Christ. With the Belt of Truth around our waist, we are prepared to defend ourselves against the enemy's deceit and lies.

THE WORD OF GOD IS TRUTH

So Jesus said to those Jews who had believed in Him, If you abide in My word [hold fast to My teachings and live in accordance with them], you are truly My disciples.

And you will know the Truth and the Truth will set you free.

__John 8:31-32(AMPC)

Psalm 119:160(ESV) says, "The sum of your word is truth, and every one of your righteous rules endures forever."

John 17:17 (ESV) says, "Sanctify them in the truth; your word is truth."

Abide means to continue or to remain. Abiding in

God's Word is a commitment we make realizing that when we know God's Word and stick with it, it will produce life-changing results in our lives. If we continue in the Truth of God's Word and refuse to give up, our lives will change dramatically.

Jesus says in Mark 4:24 (AMPC) says, "The measure [of thought and study] you give [to the truth you hear] will be the measure [of virtue and knowledge] that comes back to you."

Jesus is saying, "What you put into the Word is what you will get out of it." When you approach God's Word with an open mind and heart, you will receive revelation knowledge and a deeper understanding of His Word. God's Word will show you Truth that will help you combat the lies of the enemy. God will transform your life and set you free as you abide in His Word.

A CHRISTIAN'S BELT OF TRUTH

This first and essential piece of the armor for the Christian in this spiritual war is the belt of Truth. To stand strong in battle, we must know the Truth of God's Word and live by that Truth. Only then will the remainder of our armor stay on, and we will be protected in this battle.

This is because, as we have learned, the belt of Truth

keeps the breastplate tight and secure. The breastplate keeps the tunic up and out of your way, so you won't get trapped up or slowed down. It also gives you a place to keep your sword.

Without Truth, we are easily deceived by Satan's lies. Satan's lies are the things that destroy our relationships, our lives, and our futures. Remember, one little lie was what Satan used in the Garden of Eden to destroy the future of all humanity. How can we put on the belt of Truth? Paul does say several times in the previous verses to put on the armor of God. How do we put on this first piece of the armor, the belt of Truth? How do we recognize the Truth and live by it?

You must buckle up the belt of Truth around your waist, so you can stand strong in the Truth of God's Word. Putting on the belt of Truth is gaining knowledge of the Bible and applying that Truth to our lives.

GOD'S BELT

This belt of Truth is God's belt. In *Isaiah 11:5(NKJV),* Tells us that righteousness will be the belt of God's loins and faithfulness the belt of His waist.

Righteousness shall be the belt of His loins, And faithfulness the belt around his waist.

__Isaiah 11:5 (NKJV)

14

First, we must understand that the belt of Truth is not our belt. It's God's belt of Truth. The Truth that we are to buckle around ourselves is God's Truth. God's Truth is His Word. *Psalm 119:160* tells us that God's Word is Truth. In *John 17:17*, praying to God, Jesus said, "*Your Word is Truth.*"

In *Colossians 1:5 (KJV)*, Paul calls the Bible specifically the Gospel message, "*The Word of Truth.*" Similarly, in *2 Timothy 2:15 (KJV)*, we are told as Christians to divide the "*Word of Truth*" rightly. This is what it boils down to: If we want to put on this first piece of spiritual armor, we need to delve into God's Word.

In *Proverbs 6:21-23 (NKJV)*, we are told by King Solomon, the wisest man who ever lived, that to live the good life comes from taking the Truth of God's Word and binding it on our hearts, and tying it around our neck; thinking about it when we walk, when we sleep, and when we wake up.

Therefore, we put on the belt of Truth by putting on the Word of God. So putting on the belt is immersing yourself in the Word of God. This is done by reading and studying the Bible, listening to teachers and preachers who teach the Bible, and meditating on scripture verses.

Putting on the Truth of God's Word is putting on the belt of Truth. Then, only in this way, when you have put it on, will you be able to use it as a piece of armor in battle. Putting on the first piece of armor, the belt of Truth, is your first step on your journey to victorious living and winning your battles in life.

CHAPTER 3

THE BREASTPLATE OF RIGHTEOUSNESS

With the breastplate of righteousness in place,

__Ephesians 6:14 (NIV)

The breastplate's purpose was to protect the soldier's vital organs from his neck to his waist. If the soldier did not wear his breastplate, an arrow could easily reach his chest, piercing his heart or lungs. The breastplate protected the soldier when he was not quick enough to take up his shield.

As Believers, we only have the righteousness that has been given to us by God. Our breastplate is His righteousness, and His righteousness will never fail. Even though we don't have any righteousness of our own, we must still, by His power, choose to live right. Living a righteous life, rooted in God's Word, is powerful in protecting our hearts and defeating the enemy. Without righteousness, we are opened up for the enemy's attack.

In *Isaiah 59*, the Lord puts on *"righteousness as a breastplate"* and goes to battle against injustice and corruption. He restores peace and order to the land.

Righteousness comes from faith in Jesus Christ. God offers His own righteousness to every Believer in Jesus Christ. Righteousness is not gained by doing good deeds. Instead, it comes from faith in Jesus Christ.

PUTTING ON THE BREASTPLATE OF RIGHTEOUSNESS MEANS:

1. Standing firm against injustice and corruption. *(Leviticus 19:15; Hebrews 1:9)*

2. Believing in Jesus and His Righteousness, not our own righteousness. *(Galatians 2:20, 21)*

3. Knowing God promises His protection against the forces of evil for those who have faith in Jesus. *(2 Thessalonians 3:3)*

RIGHTEOUSNESS BY GRACE

Romans 3:21-23(KJV) says,

But now the righteousness of God without the law is manifested, being witnessed by the law and the prophets;

Even the righteousness of God which is by faith of Jesus Christ unto all and upon all them that believe: for there is no difference:

For all have sinned, and come short of the glory of God;

This righteousness is for everyone who believes. We have to receive it by faith in Jesus Christ. This righteousness of God is apart from the Law. We cannot do anything to earn it. Notice in *verse 22* that God's righteousness is through faith in Jesus Christ unto all and upon all those who believe. God offers His righteousness to everyone because the Bible says, *"For all have sinned, and come short of the glory of God."*

We were born sinners, and we need a Savior. We all do not measure up to God's standard or perfection. Because of our sin, the most significant thing we need is right standing with God, and God has offered this through faith in Jesus Christ, not through the works of the law.

The Bible says Abraham believed God. He believed the promise God gave him, and then righteousness was assigned to his account. Abraham was declared righteous before God through his faith.

Romans 3:21-22 (NIV) says, "But now apart from the law the righteousness of God has been made known, to which the Law and the Prophets testify.

This righteousness is given through faith in Jesus Christ to all who believe. There is no difference between Jew and Gentile.

19

These verses let us know that because of the payment Jesus made on the cross when He shed His blood for our sins, righteousness *(right standing)* will be credited to any person's account who believes upon Christ.

Romans 5:17(KJV) says, "For if by one man's offence death reigned by one; much more they which receive abundance of grace and of the gift of righteousness shall reign in life by one, Jesus Christ."

THE GIFT OF RIGHTEOUSNESS

Righteousness means right standing with God, and to be righteous is to be in right relationship with God. Righteousness also means being or doing what is right. There are two sides to righteousness – the being side and the doing side.

Righteousness is attributed or given to everyone who trusts in Jesus Christ for the forgiveness of their sins. This means that God has done even more than forgive your sins through Jesus Christ. He has also put righteousness into your account, like when someone anonymous puts money into your bank account.

The righteousness now belongs to you. Nobody can take it away from you. Even Satan can't take it away. Once you are saved, Satan can't do anything to change your righteous standing before God.

As Christians, we want to be in right relationship with

God, but most of us try to obtain righteousness by our own efforts. We need to realize that to become righteous; we need to put our faith in what Jesus has already done for us.

If we attempt to become righteous by doing anything else, such as by trying to be good or doing good things, we will not succeed. Righteousness is a free gift, and if we try to earn it ourselves, it's in effect saying, "What Jesus did wasn't enough. I have to do something more myself!"

We became righteous when we were born again. As we put our faith in what Jesus has done for us, the righteousness Jesus obtained by His faith becomes ours. At new birth, our spirits are changed to be like God's Spirit and receive the righteousness of God Himself. The following are important facts about the breastplate of righteousness:

HOW CAN THE SPIRITUAL BREASTPLATE BE USED FOR THE CHRISTIAN IN SPIRITUAL BATTLE?

The breastplate of righteous, which is attached to the belt of Truth, applies the Truth of God's Word to our lives. The belt of Truth comes first because there can't be righteousness without Truth. To know that something is right, you need to know that it is true.

The breastplate is to get the Truth of God, not only

strapped around us like the belt of Truth, not just so we can quote scripture, but to get the Truth of God inside us, protect our vital organs from damage, and to live according to the Truth of God's Word.

The breastplate of righteousness applies God's Truth to our lives, to live holy and righteous before God rather than live in sin.

HOW CAN WE PUT ON THE SPIRITUAL BREASTPLATE OF RIGHTEOUSNESS?

Like the belt of Truth, we must first understand that the breastplate of righteousness is God's.

He put on righteousness as his breastplate, and the helmet of salvation on his head; he put on the garments of vengeance and wrapped himself in zeal as in a cloak.

__Isaiah 59:17 (NIV)

Just as the breastplate on a soldier protects his heart, lungs, and other vital organs, the breastplate of righteousness and living in obedience to God protects the heart of a Christian.

WHY IS PROTECTING YOUR HEART SO IMPORTANT?

An important thing to know about the breastplate of righteousness is what it is designed to protect–the heart.

Because your heart is what makes the rest of your body work, if the heart stops, everything stops. The heart is incredibly important.

Proverbs 4:23 (NIV) says, Above all else, guard your heart, for everything you do flows from it.

The heart is a physical pump that controls the flow of blood throughout the body. Your spiritual heart, your essence, your core, and the thing that makes you, *you* is the pump that God uses to fill you with new life. Do you remember that once you trust Christ for your salvation, you were made new with His righteousness?

2 Corinthians 5:17 (NIV) says, "Therefore, if anyone is in Christ, the new creation has come: The old has gone, the new is here!"

CHAPTER 4

THE SHOES OF THE GOSPEL OF PEACE

And with your feet fitted with the readiness that comes from the gospel of peace.

__Ephesians 6:15 (NIV)

The Roman soldier's shoes were made from thick leather. The shoes were studded through the soles with hobnails, which enabled the soldier to stand firm. *A hobnail is a short large-headed nail for studding shoe soles (Webster).*

The studs kept the soldier's feet from slipping when he was in battle. This helped him have a firm foundation. Without his shoes, a Roman soldier would not be able to maintain his position against his enemies.

Christians also have a firm foundation in the gospel. As Believers in Christ, we have peace in knowing we are secure in what Jesus has done for us. In the gospel, we are prepared for all kinds of difficulties. The gospel gives us the stability for sure footing, allowing us to march over the rough terrain of life without giving up. We must be prepared to share the gospel of peace at any time.

The gospel of peace keeps our feet anchored and

standing firm and strong. It is the good news of the gospel that we can have peace with God. We can also have peace with ourselves and with others. Before we turned to Jesus, we had a desire to live only for ourselves. We did not care about God's will for our lives. But God loves us and made a way for us to be reconciled with Him and live in peace.

THE WORD PEACE HAS TWO MEANINGS:

1. *Absence of conflict among each other.* God wants Believers to live in peace and unity with one another. *(1 Thessalonians 5:13 (NIV)*

2. *Absence of worry and anxiety.* This peace is the confidence that God has everything under control.

HOW TO USE THE SHOES OF THE GOSPEL OF PEACE?

Ephesians 6:15 (NIV) says, "And with your feet fitted with the readiness that comes from the gospel of peace."

How can the gospel of peace be compared to shoes? First, what is the gospel of peace? As stated, the word *gospel* means *good news* referring to the sacrifice Jesus made for us to be saved. This *good news* gives us peace.

With God's strength and power, we can be courageous in sharing our faith with others. Jesus has already defeated death, so we do not need to be afraid. Our shoes equip us to walk through difficult, rocky, and unsmooth areas. In the same way, having the hope of the gospel helps us walk through the problematic adversity and trials we may face in life.

John 16:33 (ESV) says, "I have said these things to you, that in me you may have peace. In the world you will have tribulation. But take heart; I have overcome the world."

Having a good pair of shoes can help us walk across rugged terrain, wearing the shoes of the gospel of peace prepares us to share the gospel of Jesus Christ boldly with others. Having our feet fitted with the shoes of the readiness of the gospel of peace will help us be ready to share the good news of the gospel with others at all times. We should always be prepared to share Christ with others because a person's decision to follow Christ is one of the most important decisions he or she will ever make.

PEACE IN THE STORM

You keep him in perfect peace whose mind is stayed on you, because he trusts in you.

Miranda Burnette

__Isaiah 26:3 ESV

Peace is freedom from disquieting or oppressive thoughts or emotions. (Webster) God wants us to keep our minds on Him when we face challenges in our lives. We shouldn't focus and dwell on the problem but on God. Our help comes from the Lord, the Maker of heaven and earth *(Psalm 121:2)*. Trails come to make us strong *(1 Peter 1:7)*. The Bible tells us that, "Weeping may endure for a night, but joy comes in the morning" *(Psalm 30:5)*.

Everyone has problems! It is not as much as what happens to you, but your response to the problems that will make you stronger or cause you to give up. God will go through the storms with us. If God is right there with us, why should we fear? The acronym FEAR is widely used by many to represent False Evidence Appearing Real. This means that fear is an illusion. It is not real. Many things we believe and are fearful of are lies from the devil. Don't believe the devil's lies, but instead believe the Truth of God's Word.

The Word of God will give us God's power and peace in the storm. We need to set aside time to fill our minds with the Word of God. If we do this, when the storm comes, we can have peace that passes all understanding.

And the peace of God, which surpasses all understanding, will guard your hearts and your minds in Christ Jesus.

BE STRONG

_Philippians 4:7 ESV

The key to our peace and success is found in God's Word. Read, study, and meditate on God's Word, and it will strengthen your faith to receive God's peace and succeed in life. The Word of God will give you strength for the battles you face in life.

Stand firm in challenging times. Hold on to your peace. God is in control, and He is for you. He is on your side. So you can't help but win! *You are more than a conqueror! (Romans 8:37)*

Did you know that you can have peace in the middle of a storm? Did you know that it's in these exact moments when true peace wins the battle? That is because even though you are experiencing chaos on the outside, God's peace on the inside can totally calm your mind.

In fact, the Bible says that the peace of God is the opposite of the natural way we respond to life's problems that we often can't understand it!

Philippians 4:7 (NIV) says, "And the peace of God, which transcend all understanding, will guard your hearts and your minds in Christ Jesus."

God gives you a peace that is far beyond what you can understand. When you receive and walk in His peace, your heart and mind are settled as you rely on Him.

FINDING GOD'S PEACE IN THE MIDST OF THE STORM

John 16:33 (NIV) tells us, "I have told you these things, so that in me you may have peace. In this world you will have trouble. But take heart! I have overcome the world."

Everyone goes through storms. But when the storms of life actually come, how will you respond? Will you lose your peace, worry, and get anxious?

Philippians 4:6 (NIV) tells us, "Do not be anxious about anything, but in every situation, by prayer and petition, with thanksgiving, present your requests to God."

There are many kinds of storms. You may be experiencing a financial storm. You may be in a complicated relationship at this time. Your health may not be in the best shape.

There may be problems on your job, or you may need employment. It doesn't matter what type of storm you are going through right now. You can experience an *inner* peace that isn't dependent on *outer* circumstances. What can we do when the storms come? How do we stand against them?

WHAT TO DO WHEN THE STORMS COME?

BE STRONG

1. WHEN THE STORMS COME: STAND ON THE WORD OF GOD

Sometimes people wonder, "Why should I spend so much time reading, studying, and meditating on God's Word? This is why. When the storm comes: when discouragement, disappointment, despair, hurt and pain, and suffering are clouding your mind, those verses that you've hidden in your heart will start coming out of your mouth.

Besides, God's Word will give you peace in the middle of the storm. Don't be moved by what you see with your natural eyes. Be moved by God's Word.

Matthew 14:28-30 (NIV) says, "Lord, if it's you," Peter replied, "tell me to come to you on the water." "Come," he said. Then Peter got down out of the boat, walked on the water and came toward Jesus. But when he saw the wind, he was afraid and, beginning to sink, cried out, "Lord, save me!"

Do you realize that when Peter stepped out on the water to walk toward Jesus, he wouldn't have started sinking if he had kept his eyes on the Lord? Nevertheless, what did he do? He let the circumstances around him, the wind rising, waves roaring, and the storm raging, cause fear to arise in his heart. Then he began to fear; he lost his peace. When he lost his peace, he started to sink.

The same thing could be true for your life. When you keep your eyes focused on the Word of God, His Word will help you walk on top of the circumstances. However, if you begin to focus on your troubles and problems, you're going to sink.

Proverb 4:22 (NIV) says, "For they are life to those who find them and health to one's whole body."

Take the medicine of God's Word. The medicine of God's Word will heal your body. It will heal your emotions, it will heal your mind, it will heal and restore your relationships, it will heal your home, and it will heal your marriage. Moreover, when you take the medicine of God's Word, there will be no harmful side effects. You will just have God's perfect peace. Trust in the Lord and acknowledge Him, lean, and depend on God.

Trust in the Lord with all your heart and lean not on your own understanding; In all your ways submit to Him, and he will make your paths straight.

__Proverbs 3:5-6 (NIV)

2. WHEN THE STORMS COME: HAVE FAITH IN GOD

Mark 11:22-24 (NIV), "Have faith in God," Jesus answered. "Truly I tell you, if anyone says to this mountain, 'Go, throw yourself into the sea,' and does not doubt in their heart but believes that what they say will happen, it will be done for them. Therefore I tell you, whatever you ask for in prayer, believe that you have received it, and it will be yours.

Speak the Word. Just like Jesus spoke to the storm, and it obeyed him. We can do the same thing.

Mark 4:39-41 (NIV), He got up, rebuked the wind and said to the waves, "Quiet! Be still!" Then the wind died down and it was completely calm. He said to his disciples, "Why are you so afraid? Do you still have no faith?" They were terrified and asked each other, "Who is this? Even the wind and the waves obey him!"

For in it the righteousness of God is revealed from faith to faith: as it is written, The just shall live by faith.

__Romans 1:17 (KJV)

Who are the just? If you're saved, you're one of the *just.* As one of the *just,* you must learn to live by faith. Faith is a key to peace. Faith is powerful! If you are going to live in peace, rather than being anxious, stressed out, and fearful when trouble comes, you're going to do it with your faith. Faith and victory go hand and hand. They are inseparable.

We are living in unsettling, unimaginable times. In these crucial times, knowing how to operate in faith is essential. That is why you must start developing your faith. We will experience trouble in our lives at times.

But in John 16:33 (NIV) Jesus said, "I have told you these things, so that in me you may have peace. In this world you will have trouble. But take heart! I have overcome the world.

3. WHEN THE STORMS COME: CAST YOUR CARES UPON THE LORD

1Peter 5:7 (NKJV) says, "Casting all your care upon him, for he cares for you."

The Bible tells us to cast all our cares upon God. What is care? The Greek word translated care in 1 Peter 5:7 means, *"To draw in different directions, distract hence signifies 'that which causes this, care, especially an anxious care'" (Vines Expository Dictionary).*

The whole purpose of care is to distract us from our fellowship with God. That is why it is vital for us to cast our care. Cares will blind us to God's peace. When we cast our cares upon the Lord, the peace will flow.

If we want to experience God's peace in our lives, we must learn to cast all our cares upon Him and *let them stay there.* So let the peace of God flow in your life.

PEACE IS YOUR UMPIRE

Colossians 3:15 (AMPC) says, "And let the peace (soul harmony which comes) from Christ rule (act as umpire continually) in your hearts [deciding and settling with finality all questions that arise in your minds, in that peaceful state] to which as [members of Christ's] one body you were also called [to live]. And be thankful (appreciative), [giving praise to God always]."

The *Greek* word for *rule* comes from the root word from which we get our English word umpire, which means to govern or arbitrate. Govern means to rule over by right of authority *(Dictionary.com).* Arbitrate means to decide between opposing or contending parties or sides *(Dictionary.com).* Peace is to be our umpire. What is the primary job of a baseball umpire?

We can understand this in the same way we understand the function of an umpire in baseball: The umpire in a ball game decides if you are in or out of the game. Once the umpire makes the call, it is decided. His decision is final. If he calls a pitch a ball, it is a ball. If he calls a runner out, the runner is out.

In the same way, peace should be the umpire in your life that decides if something should be in your life or out. The peace of God should act just like an umpire in our hearts, deciding which opportunities we should act on and which ones we should let pass by. The game is centered on what the umpire calls. His word is the rule.

Likewise, the peace of God is to make the call in your life. You have a lot of choices to make in life. What job to take? Where to move or which house to buy? Where to send your children to school? Should you go back to college? When we follow peace instead of being led by our emotions, we will make good choices and wise decisions.

The Bible instructs us to let God's peace call the shots, make the decisions, and rule our emotions. When you have a choice to make, whether big or small, be led by peace. You need to go in the direction you have the most peace.

Natural peace is only experienced in the absence of problems. God has given us His supernatural peace to enjoy. God's peace is independent of circumstances. Many people are looking for peace today in every place but the right place, which is in the Lord.

Some try to find peace in possessions, pleasure, or pills. They are turning to drugs and alcohol to help them find peace. They discover too late that drugs and alcohol can only give temporary peace, but only God can give us lasting peace, which only comes through Jesus Christ.

You can have peace no matter what is happening on your job, in your home, or in the world around you. Start today, enjoying a life of peace by casting your cares upon the Lord, and receiving His peace in your life.

CHAPTER 5

THE SHIELD OF FAITH

In addition to all this, take up the shield of faith, with which you can extinguish all the flaming arrows of the evil one.

__Ephesians 6:16 (NIV)

The Roman soldiers would drench their leather-covered shields with water before going into battle. When the fiery arrows of their enemies hit those soaked shields, the flames were immediately extinguished.

A Roman soldier's shield was huge. It was about two and a half to three feet wide and four feet long. It was big for a reason. In the heat of the battle, the soldier could crouch down and hide behind his shield when the enemy was shooting arrows at him.

The verb shield means to protect or to cover. God has given you the shield of faith to protect you from the enemy. The shield of faith is the Believer's protection against temptation. Whenever we trust that God loves us and will provide everything we need, we cannot be tempted to give up and trust in the wrong sources to meet our needs. God is our source.

When faced with genuine faith in God, the powers of darkness are overcome. That is why the Apostle John could say, *"This is the victory that has overcome the world even our faith"* (1 John 5:4).

The shield was the soldier's primary defensive weapon. Faith is the shield of the Believer. Trusting God's power and protection is crucial in remaining steadfast. When the battle is raging, we must remember that God works all things for good *(Romans 8:28).* He is always faithful to His promises.

FIGHT THE GOOD FIGHT OF FAITH

Fight the good fight of faith. Lay hold on eternal life, to which you are called and have professed a good profession before many witnesses.

__ 1 Timothy 6:12 (MEV)

Sometimes we have to fight! We have to fight the good fight of faith. It is called the "good" fight because that's the fight we win! We always win with God! It is also called the "good" fight of faith because God fights for us and through us. We don't have to fight this fight in our own strength.

In this fight of faith, we are fighting the enemy of

unbelief. The enemy of unbelief often comes to us to try to get us to doubt the things God is speaking to us, through His *"Written Word"* or through a *"Rhema Word."* A Rhema is "The Spoken Word." God will not speak a word that contradicts His written Word.

If the devil comes against you with unbelief, you need to let that enemy know that, *"If God said it, I believe, and that settles it."* God gives us the power to defeat the enemy of unbelief.

Romans 10:17 (MEV) goes on to say, "So then faith comes by hearing, and hearing by the Word of God."

So if the enemy of doubt or unbelief is coming against you, strengthen your faith muscles with the Word of God. Put on the whole armor of God *(Ephesians 6:10-18)*, and hold up your shield of faith and the sword of the spirit which is the Word of God, and fight the good fight of faith and win. You can't lose with God on your side. You have the victory!

And above all, taking the shield of faith, with which you will be able to extinguish all the fiery arrows of the evil one.

__ Ephesians 6:16 (MEV)

The Bible tells us to fight the good fight of faith. We are strong soldiers in the army of the Lord! The main purpose of an army is to ensure liberty and freedom.

Without this freedom, we would have to live under someone else's rule and authority. In the spiritual world, the battle over world rule has already been fought and won by our Lord Jesus Christ.

As Christians, we are not defeated no matter what the circumstances look like. In *2 Corinthians 2:14 (KJV)*, The Apostle Paul said, *"My God always causes me to triumph in Christ Jesus."*

Before soldiers go into battle, they must be adequately trained and equipped. If God calls us to do something, He will equip us to do it. He will not send us into battle without preparing us first. Before any soldier receives an assignment, he or she must go through a course of training. God will not send us out into the heat of the battle unequipped.

During this time of training, the soldier will go through a very rigorous mental and physical time of training. The major purpose of this training is to get them prepared and ready to fight. The training prepared them to be properly equipped so they would be able to do what was required of them to get the job done even under the harshest environment. There is a reason the Apostle Paul compared Christians to soldiers. A Christian in God's army, just like a soldier in the military, must be prepared to do battle by being fully trained and equipped to fight.

Trained soldiers stand strong! They don't allow fear to dominate them. They will have learned during the training, how to stand strong, and do battle. This training is required to be victorious.

I admonish you to put on the full armor of God and begin to stand firm and fight those battles against your enemies who will try to defeat you and your loved ones. Be strong and courageous! We must keep our faith built up so that we will have *endurance* when the fight comes. A soldier without endurance is a soldier who will give up in a time of battle. Endurance is the ability to withstand hardship or adversity *(Webster)*.

2 Timothy 2:3 (NKJV) says, "You therefore must endure hardship as a good soldier of Jesus Christ."

This verse lets us know that we have the ability to *endure;* therefore, we can. We can do all things through Christ, who gives us the strength and power. We can be confident and sure that we will come out victoriously when we build ourselves up in the Word of God.

Faith obtains what God has already provided. As children of God, we already have all the faith we're ever going to need to acquire anything God has or is going to do for us *(Romans 12:3 ESV)*. Jesus said in *Matthew 17:20,* "Faith the size of a mustard seed could move a mountain." You don't need more faith; you need more Word.

God has already given you enough strength to fight and equipped you with the weapons and armor you need. You just need the shield of faith.

We have gone through this training and preparation, so our faith would not fail but stay strong in times of trials and adversity. So keep the faith and STAY STRONG!

Just as a small fire is extinguished by the storm whereas a large fire is enhanced by it – likewise a weak faith is weakened by predicament and catastrophes whereas a strong faith is strengthened by them."

__Viktor E. Frankl

WE CAN RELEASE THE POWER IN FAITH BY OUR WORDS

In the spiritual world, words are carriers of faith, and a spiritual law, according to Jesus, is that we receive in life what we believe.

Jesus said to him, If you can believe, all things are possible to him who believes.

Mark 9:23 (NKJV)

Speak words of faith instead of doubt and unbelief. Jesus said we could speak to a mountain, and if we really believed in our words, it would be removed and thrown into the sea. He said we would have what we say.

Truly I tell you, if anyone says to this mountain, 'Go, throw yourself into the sea,' and does not doubt in their heart but believes that what they say will happen, it will be done for them.

Mark 11:23 (NIV)

We can have what we say if we say it with our mouths and believe it in our hearts. The words that are filled with faith are the words that have power. To have what we say, we have to mix faith with our words, and believe those words, from our hearts. You can release your faith through words. You will have what you say if what you say is spoken in faith.

THE PROMISES OF GOD ARE VOICE ACTIVATED

That means you have to say something, and what you say has to line up with the Word of God. Words are faith containers. Our words carry what we believe from our hearts into our lives. That is the awesome power of speaking God's Word. Anything that will produce positive results in our lives, the enemy will try to fight against it. So hold on to your confession in the middle of adversity. As you hold on to your confession, you develop your faith muscles, and your faith becomes stronger and stronger and more effective.

FAITH: THE TITLE DEED

Hebrews 11:1 (AMP) states the definition of faith:

Now faith is the assurance (TITLE DEED, confirmation) of things hoped for (divinely guaranteed), and the EVIDENCE of things not seen [the conviction of their reality—faith comprehends as fact what cannot be experienced by the physical senses].

A *title deed* is a document that states and proves a person's legal right to own a piece of land or a building *(Cambridge Dictionary).* If I showed you the deed to my house, you wouldn't question if there really was a house at that address. You can't see the house, but my title deed is enough proof that it exists, and it is mine.

According to *Hebrews 11:1,* faith is our *title deed,* and we are the legal owners of those things we are hoping for. What are you hoping for? Are you hoping for physical or emotional healing? Our title deed states in *1 Peter 2:24 (BSB) He Himself bore our sins in His body on the tree, so that we might die to sin and live to righteousness. "By His stripes, you are healed."*

Are you hoping for a promotion on your job to pay your bills and stop the collection calls? Our title deed states in *Philippians 4:19 (KJV), "But my God shall supply all your need according to his riches in glory by Christ Jesus."*

Are you hoping for a restored marriage? Our title deed

44

states in *Luke 1:37 (AMP)*, *"For with God nothing [is or ever] shall be impossible."* Are you hoping for God's protection? Our title deed states in *Psalm 91:10 (NKJV)*, *"No evil shall befall you, Nor shall any plague come near your dwelling;"*

Our entire justice system is based on evidence. For example, when a district attorney brings you into court to accuse you of a crime, he'd better have some convincing evidence to support his claim or some other type of testimony. Otherwise, the judge is going to throw the case out of court.

The same can be said about your faith if you're going to claim that healing, provision, peace, safety, or some other blessing belonging to you, you'd better have some evidence to back it up. Go to God's Word and find a promise that speaks to your particular situation. That promise is your legal *title deed* to the promises of God that can be found in His Word.

Faith is the evidence of the things not seen. The thing might be money to pay your bills. The thing you need could be healing. The thing might be a new car. Whatever thing it is, faith is the *evidence* of that *thing.* You must realize that you are not going to receive any*thing* without faith evidence.

An unbeliever's mindset is, *"I'll believe it when I see it."* But faith is the believer's evidence that a thing is his, even though he's doesn't see it. If you can see something, you're not using faith. It's easy to believe in something you *can* see, but God wants you to have faith even when you *can't* see what you are hoping for.

No matter what you need or how severe your circumstances maybe, if you will hold on to your *title deed,* you will surely receive what you believe. Your part is to believe that God can and will help you overcome your problems and then act on that belief. Put some action with your faith. Remember, God has already given you enough power to do battle. He's already given you enough strength to fight. You just need to use the shield of faith.

CHAPTER 6

THE HELMET OF SALVATION

Take the helmet of salvation...

__Ephesians 6:17 (NIV)

The helmet worn by the Roman soldier protected his head and neck form the enemy's weapons and from falling debris. The soldier's head is an extremely vulnerable area. The soldier's helmet covered his entire head, facial area, and between the eyes.

The helmet of salvation represents Jesus' death on the cross and His resurrection from the dead, which provides all Believers with freedom from the bondage of sin and with eternal life.

The Believer's helmet of salvation is a vital piece of his armor. There is no victory without salvation. Salvation empowers Believers to fight. It protects us in our weaknesses.

What does a helmet do for you? The main purpose of a helmet—whether it's a soldier's helmet, a construction worker's hard hat, or a cyclist's helmet—is to protect the brain from injury.

For instance, a football player's helmet is padded on the inside to absorb the force when he gets pounded to the ground. The brain must be fiercely protected because once the brain becomes damaged, the body becomes damaged too.

Just as your brain is the control center for your body, your mind is the control center for your will and emotions. Your mind needs to be protected with a helmet that can absorb the force that comes from being hit by the enemy in battle.

Your mind is vitally important. What you put into it—words, images, thoughts—has a direct impact on what you do and who you become.

Proverbs 23:7 (NASB) strongly warns us to guard our minds: "As he thinks within himself, so he is."

This means, quite simply, that we *do* what we *think*. The way you think is the kind of person you will become. Many battles we deal with start in the mind. Satan attacks us on the battlefield of our minds. However, we can defeat the enemy by keeping our minds in agreement with God's Word. So get into God's Word and continue to build up your faith and renew your mind to who you are in Christ.

Protection for the head was essential to the Roman soldier as he was involved in close combat. Because of this, he wore an iron-reinforced helmet. Some had additional bronze pieces to protect the ears. The helmet was polished with oil to make the metal slick or slippery. This caused the blows of swords, war clubs, or battle-axes to be deflected upon impact.

Paul states that we have head protection for our battles, it being salvation. After accepting Jesus as your Savior, it's imperative that you study and apply God's Word to your life daily. Until this transformation occurs, your mind will still think worldly thoughts, and you will continue to fall prey to the same temptations as before.

This leads others to believe that many Christians are hypocrites, but just because an individual fails to overcome temptation doesn't mean that he or she is not a Christian. To renew our minds with the Word of God, we can read the Word, pray the Word, listen to the Word being preached, listen to the Word being taught, read books with the Word in them, and listen to the Word on mp3's or CDs. Your mind is being renewed right now by reading this book.

HOW DO WE RECEIVE SALVATION?

Accepting Jesus Christ as your Lord and Savior is the most important decision you'll ever make.

GOD'S WORD PROMISES,

"...If you confess with your mouth the Lord Jesus and believe in your heart that God has raised Him from the

dead, you will be saved."

"For with the heart one believes unto righteousness, and with the mouth confession is made unto salvation"
(Romans 10:9-10 NKJV).

For whoever calls on the name of the Lord shall be saved"
(Romans 10:13).

By His grace, God has already provided salvation. Your part is simply to *believe it* and *receive it.*

PRAY THIS PRAYER OUT LOUD

"Jesus, I accept You as my Lord and Savior.

I believe in my heart that God raised You from the dead.

By faith in Your Word, I receive salvation now.

Thank You for saving me."

If you prayed this prayer, God heard you and saved you, I personally want to welcome you to the family of God! Everyone who comes to Christ and receives salvation by faith, becomes a brand-new person. Everything old is gone, and everything is completely new. That is why Jesus referred to this experience as being born-again in *John 3:3.*

IT SAYS:

In John 3:3 (KJV), Jesus answered and said unto him, Verily, verily, I say unto thee, Except a man be born again, he cannot see the kingdom of God.

STABILITY IN AN UNSTABLE WORLD

We all need God! If you don't have God, you are standing on shaky ground, and eventually, you might sink. Like the familiar hymn says, "On Christ the solid Rock I stand, all other ground is sinking sand."

Psalm 18:2 (ESV) says, "The Lord is my rock and my fortress and my deliver, my God, my rock, in whom I take refuge, my shield, and the horn of my salvation, my stronghold."

We live in an unstable world! The world is full of uncertainty. It is constantly changing. Relationships change. We read about social injustice. People come and go. Jobs change. Employment is not steady. The political landscape is no longer stable. Turmoil is everywhere!

Numerous things can upset the balance of your life in the course of a day. But with God, even in this constantly changing, uncertain world, it is possible to find stability.

Holding firmly on to Christ provides a strong unshakable foundation amidst shaky and unstable circumstances in life. When you choose to make Christ the foundation of your life, you will find that while the instability of the world may still trip you up, and everything around you is falling apart. You will always be left standing strong on the foundation of God's Word.

Matthew 7:24-27 (NIV) says, "Therefore everyone who hears these words of mine and puts them into practice is like a wise man who built his house on the rock.

The rain came down, the streams rose, and the winds blew and beat against that house; yet it did not fall, because it had its foundation on the rock.

But everyone who hears these words of mine and does not put them into practice is like a foolish man who built his house on sand.

The rain came down, the streams rose, and the winds blew and beat against that house, and it fell with a great crash."

If you have made Jesus the Lord of your life, You might fall, but you will rise up again!

Proverbs 24:16 (AMP) says, "For a righteous man falls seven times, and rises again, But the wicked stumble in times of disaster and collapse."

Isaiah 26:4 (AMPC) says, "So trust in the Lord (commit yourself to Him, lean on Him, hope confidently in Him) forever; for the Lord God is an everlasting Rock [the Rock of Ages]."

You can stand firm on that *Everlasting Rock* because He will never let you down. He is a solid foundation you can confidently stand on. Things around you may shake, but you will not fall. If the whole world around you is unstable and shaking, you can hold on to your *Rock,* the Lord Jesus Christ. God is your reliable source of supernatural strength and power.

ON CHRIST THE SOLID ROCK WE STAND STRONG!

CHAPTER 7

THE SWORD OF THE SPIRIT

"Take ... the sword of the Spirit, which is the word of God."

__Ephesians 6:17 (NIV)

The sword is the only offensive weapon. The belt, breastplate, shoes, shield, and helmet are not offensive weapons. The purpose of the defensive weapons was to protect the soldier from the enemy. These weapons are all defensive in nature. They are protection against the forces that come against us.

The sword is designed to defeat the enemy's plan and rescue lives. The sword is a deadly weapon. With a sword, a skilled warrior could pierce through even the strongest armor. The sword of the Spirit is the Word of God. The Bible says,

"For the word of God is alive and powerful. It is sharper than the sharpest two-edged sword, cutting between soul and spirit, between joint and marrow. It exposes our innermost thoughts and desires."

__ Hebrews 4:12 (NLT)

Our sword is the Word of God. When a Christian is under attack, he can fight back with the Word of God and win. God's Word is a weapon against the enemy. A Christian equipped with the Word of God is armed and dangerous! The Word of God, also like a sword, is an offensive weapon. This is the weapon that you can use to inflict real damage on your enemy.

"A pilot without his chart, a scholar without his book, and a soldier without his sword, are alike ridiculous. But, above all these, it is absurd for one to think of being a Christian, without knowledge of the Word of God and some skill to use this weapon."

_William Gurnall, The Christian in Complete Armor

JESUS IS THE WORD

John1:1 (AMPC) says, "In the beginning [before all time] was the Word (Christ), and the Word was with God, and the Word was God Himself."

The Bible isn't just a book; it is God Himself. Everything we need can be found in the Word of God. We can find answers to all of our problems in the Word of God. The Bible, God's Holy Word, is one of our most valuable possessions. Jesus gives us a good example of the way to use the sword of the Spirit.

When the devil tempted Jesus for forty days and

nights in the wilderness, each time the devil told Jesus a lie, Jesus responded, "It is written...," and quoted a scripture that *refuted (rejected)* the lie. That is exactly what we should do when the devil attacks or tries to tempt us. We should attack the enemy, the devil, with the sword of the Spirit, which is the Word of God.

MATTHEW 4:1-11(NIV) SAYS,

Then Jesus was led by the Spirit into the wilderness to be tempted by the devil. After fasting forty days and forty nights, he was hungry. The tempter came to him and said, "If you are the Son of God, tell these stones to become bread."

Jesus answered, "It is written: 'Man shall not live on bread alone, but on every word that comes from the mouth of God.'"

Then the devil took him to the holy city and had him stand on the highest point of the temple.

"If you are the Son of God," he said, "throw yourself down. For it is written:

"'He will command his angels concerning you, and they will lift you up in their hands,

so that you will not strike your foot against a stone.'"

Jesus answered him, "It is also written: 'Do not put the

Lord your God to the test.'"

Again, the devil took him to a very high mountain and showed him all the kingdoms of the world and their splendor.

"All this I will give you," he said, "if you will bow down and worship me."

Jesus said to him, "Away from me, Satan! For it is written: 'Worship the Lord your God, and serve him only.'"

Then the devil left him, and angels came and attended him.

The Word of God is a Sword. The Word of God is the two-edged sword that is your weapon of offense with which you can defend yourself. It is sharp, quick, and a two-edged sword. It exposes true motives, thoughts, purposes, and intents. It shows us the reality of ourselves. Others might see what nice things we are doing for someone, but the Word of God reveals why we are doing it. The Word of God is alive, and it has the power to change you. The Word of God will also give you strength. The Word of God will strengthen you.

Psalm 119: 28 says, "My soul dissolves because of grief; renew and strengthen me according to [the promises of] Your word."

The Word of God will give us the strength we need not

to give up. God's Word will also give us strength to not yield to temptation. It will give us the strength we need to walk in love and forgive others who mistreat us.

God's Word will give you the strength you need to handle any situation that you have to face. The word of God will recharge your batteries and give you the strength you need to press on in the name of Jesus in any circumstance. The Word of God strengthens under challenging times and afflictions.

Proverbs 18:14 (AMPC) says, "The strong spirit of a man sustains him in bodily pain or trouble, but a weak and broken spirit who can raise up or bear?"

This can happen if we eat the Word or feed ourselves spiritually. Studying the Word of God and becoming strong spiritually, will sustain you in a time of trouble.

THE WORD OF GOD HAS THE POWER TO CHANGE YOU

All of us, with no covering on our faces, show the shining-greatness of the Lord as in a mirror. All the time we are being changed to look like Him, with more and more of His shining-greatness. This change is from the Lord Who is the Spirit.

__ 2 Corinthians 3:18 (NLV)

God's Word will change you! The Word of God is powerful. As previously stated, *Hebrews 4:12* tells us that the Word of God is full of power and is sharper than a two-edged sword.

The Word of God will stand. Everything is going down, but the Word of God. *Isaiah 40:8 (NLT) says, "The grass withers and the flowers fade, but the word of our God stands forever."* So believe and stand on God's Word.

When we meditate, ponder, study, think on, and roll God's Word over and over in our minds, God's Word will begin to work in our lives powerfully. When we get God's Word on the inside of us, good things start to happen. We think differently. When we think differently by allowing the Word of God to renew our minds, we are set free because many times, we are prisoners of our own thinking. The Word of God is the *key* that will unlock the door to the prison of your mind.

Do not be conformed to this world, but be transformed by the renewing of your mind, that you may prove what is the good and acceptable and perfect will of God.

__ Romans 12:2 (MEV)

Transformed in this verse means changed. If we just put the Word on the inside of us, our lives would change for the better. When you begin to apply the principles of God's Word to your life, you and others will begin to see your life change.

God's Word is healing and health to our bodies *(Proverbs 4:20-22 (AMP).* God's Word will be a lamp to your feet and a light to your path *(Psalm 119:105).* The Word of God will help your emotions to be stable *(Psalm 91:1).* It will keep you from sin *(Psalm 119:11).*

The Word of God will help you be prosperous, deal wisely, and be successful *(Joshua 1:8).* The Word of God will strengthen you to difficulties and afflictions *(Proverbs 18:14).* The Word of God will give you hope *(Psalm 130: 5).* Most of all, the Word of God has the power to save your soul *(Romans 1:16).* We need to plant the Word deep within our hearts. As you study and meditate on the Word of God, you are planting Word Seeds in your heart that will one day spring forth into great abundant fruit in your life.

When we face different situations in our lives, the first thing we should ask is, "What does the Word of God say about this situation?" God's Word is His will. It is God's will for His children to be happy, successful, prosperous, saved, healed, delivered, and set free. Jesus came so that we might have life and have it in abundance to the full until it overflows.

The thief comes only in order to steal and kill and destroy. I came that they may have and enjoy life, and have it in abundance [to the full, till it overflows.]

__ John 10:10 (AMP)

Reading, studying, and meditating on God's Word and allowing it to saturate you; changes your attitude, emotions, finances, health, and thinking. If you would take the Word of God and meditate on it day and night, it would change you. We need to believe God's Word and act upon it and begin to live a victorious life.

CHAPTER 8

A CHALLENGE TO STAND FIRM

Be on your guard; stand firm in the faith; be courageous; be strong.

__ 1 Corinthians 16:13

Have you ever been dared by someone to do something? I'm sure you have, even if it was when you were a child. Children are always daring one another to do something. When someone dares you to do something, it is usually not something that is very easy to do. There is typically risk or danger involved. Also, when someone dares you to do something, it makes you want to do it even more. You want to do it to prove to that person that you are capable of doing whatever he or she is challenging you to do.

As Christians, we are faced with challenges each day. We go through difficult trials. We are also faced with the problems of life. We may have problems on our job, in school, with our family, or with our finances. Whatever the problem may be, we are challenged to stand amid the trials. We are challenged to keep the faith and not to let the circumstances overcome us.

We are challenged to hold on when it seems like we can't make it, when it looks as though you just can't take it anymore, or when you've come to the end of your rope and about to give up. The Lord wants me to tell you, if you are about to give up, "Don't give up!" Your help is on the way. You are challenged to stand firm!

The word *challenge* means to dare to confront boldly. It is a contest demand. It also means to defy, which is to challenge someone to do something considered impossible. *Stand* means to endure or undergo successfully. It means to remain unchanged. *Firm* means securely fixed in place, not weak or uncertain, having a solid or compact structure that resists stress or pressure.

So don't stop believing God now! You've come too far to turn around. Stress will always be in our lives. From studying, I have learned that when it comes to stress, what happens to you is not what determines the effect of stress on your life, but how you respond to it. Stress is the response of your mind, your emotions, and your body to whatever demands made upon you.

As for pressure, we have so many responsibilities, so many things to do. We are so busy sometimes that it seems like things are pressing in upon us. We know trials come only to make us strong. We have to go through the fiery trials. But listen to what God's Word says.

BE STRONG

When you cross deep rivers, I will be with you, and you won't drown. When you walk through fire, you won't be burned or scorched by the flames.

__ Isaiah 43:2 (CEV)

If we go through the fire, we will come forth as pure gold, solid, compact, through and through, able to withstand the stress and pressures of life. *Firm* also means not easily moved or disturbed. If we are firmly fixed in place, we will be able to stand our ground when stress comes our way. We will respond to it appropriately.

When pressure is all around us, it won't press in upon us and destroy us by causing us to lose hope and give up. We will stand because we are steadfast and unmovable. We are standing firm!

1 Corinthians 15:58 (NLT) says, "So, my dear brothers and sisters, be strong and immovable. Always work enthusiastically for the Lord, for you know that nothing you do for the Lord is ever useless."

2 Corinthians 11:24-28 (NLT) states,

"Five different times the Jewish leaders gave me thirty-nine lashes.

Three times I was beaten with rods. Once I was stoned. Three times I was shipwrecked. Once I spent a whole night and a day adrift at sea.

I have traveled on many long journeys. I have faced danger from rivers and from robbers. I have faced danger from my own people, the Jews, as well as from the Gentiles. I have faced danger in the cities, in the deserts, and on the seas. And I have faced danger from men who claim to be believers but are not.

I have worked hard and long, enduring many sleepless nights. I have been hungry and thirsty and have often gone without food. I have shivered in the cold, without enough clothing to keep me warm.

Then, besides all this, I have the daily burden of my concern for all the churches."

We can see in this passage of scripture that Paul was also challenged to stand firm. Paul is giving us a summary of his sufferings. We know that Paul underwent many hardships and sufferings. He endured more than most men could take. His life was characterized by a love for the truth, which allowed no compromise for self-interest.

Having understood his duty, he followed it without pulling back or turning aside because of possible consequences to himself. Paul did not give up when things got tough. The secret of his success was that he was possessed and empowered by Christ. He was an extraordinary sufferer for Christ. We, as Christians, are also challenged as Paul was challenged.

1 Peter 4:12 (MEV) says, "Beloved, do not be surprised at the fiery ordeal that is taking place among you to test you, as though some strange thing happened to you.

Though the trials are sharp and fiery, yet they are designed only to try, not to ruin us. But as we go through trials, we should have the right attitude.

James 1:2-4 (MEV) says, "My brother, count it all joy when you fall into diverse temptations, knowing that the trying of your faith develops patience. But let patience perfect its work, that you may be perfect and complete, lacking nothing.

When the storm begins to rage, and when the winds start to blow, when the rain is pouring in your life, all you can do sometimes is to stand right there in the midst of it all and praise the Lord. You can't go to the left or the right because troubles are all around you. All you have to do is to stand firm right there and praise the Lord. Praise Him, because while you are praising Him, He is working it all out for you. Just stand still and see the salvation of the Lord.

We *can* have a victorious life! We can make it. We can take it. We can do all things through Christ, who gives us strength *(Philippians 4:13)*. The Lord won't put any more on you than you can bear. *1 Corinthians 10:13* tells us that God is faithful, and He will not allow us to be tempted beyond what we can bear.

We are more than conquerors. A *conqueror* is a winner. We are winners! A conqueror is a master of the situation, a champion, an overcomer. *To conquer* is to be victorious, to overcome, or to get the victory.

But we are *more than conquerors!* We have surpassing victory! We have that victory that is above and beyond the ordinary victory. We also have the Lord on our side. If God is for us, who can be against us? *(Romans 8:31)* We know that there is nothing too hard for God. So I challenge you today to stand firm in the Lord, no matter what comes your way or what you are going through. I DARE YOU TO STAND FIRM because you are a winner!

PRAYER IS A WEAPON

Ephesians 6:18 (AMPC) tells us to – Pray at all times (on every occasion, in every season) in the Spirit, with all [manner of] prayer and entreaty. To that end keep alert and watch with strong purpose and perseverance, interceding in behalf of all the saints (God's consecrated people).

Prayer is our most powerful weapon! It is a powerful weapon we can use against the enemy! We are *prayer warriors!* We can go to war and battle for someone while in prayer in our *war room!*

A *war room* is a private place where you go daily and intercede for others in prayer. Have you found a place of prayer? Do you have a *war room?* This is a place where we wage spiritual war against the enemy on our knees before God. Jesus calls us to our *war room* of prayer in,

Matthew 6:6 (CSB) Jesus said, "But when you pray, go into your private room, shut your door, and pray to your Father who is in secret. And your Father who sees in secret will reward you."

There are various types of prayer. Thinking we have to be in a particular posture or place and thinking that there is only one type of prayer can cause a lack of prayer. We can pray anywhere – the instruction in *Ephesians 10:18* is: *"Pray at all times, on every occasion, in every season."*

I can pray sitting, standing, or lying down. I can pray out loud or silently. I can pray while moving or being still. I can pray in public places – shopping, waiting for an appointment, in a business meeting, doing household chores, driving in my car, and so forth.

We offer various types of prayer that are proper and suited for different occasions and seasons. A joyful season will require one type of prayer, while a sorrowful one will require another. When I have a need, one type of prayer is required, when someone I know has a need, another type of prayer is required.

THE FOLLOWING LIST CONSISTS OF DIFFERENT TYPES OF PRAYER:

PRAISE, WORSHIP, AND THANKSGIVING

Praise, worship, and thanksgiving are a form of prayer because each of them is how we communicate with God.

PRAYER OF PETITION

A Petition is making a request or asking.

THE PRAYER OF COMMITMENT

When we commit an issue or a person to God, we give it or the person we are praying for to Him.

THE PRAYER OF CONSECRATION

We should regularly consecrate ourselves to God. We should give ourselves to God. This means to be set aside for God's purpose and use in prayer.

PRAYER OF PERSEVERANCE

Perseverance is a prayer that keeps on praying and does not give up.

THE PRAYER OF AGREEMENT

The prayer of agreement is two or more people praying together in agreement.

THE PRAYER OF INTERCESSION

Intercession is one of the most necessary forms of prayer. Because many people don't know how to pray for themselves, they need someone to "stand in the gap" for them.

What does standing in the gap mean? It means there is a gap (space or distance) between the person you are praying for and God, and they need someone with faith and a relationship with God to get in the gap and bring them and God together. People still have to choose God, but our intercession opens the door for God to work. In the *Book of Ezekiel 22:29-31,* God did not want to destroy the wicked people, but He could find no man to stand in the gap and pray for them.

Ezekiel 22:29-31 (AMPC)

The people of the land have used oppression and extortion and have committed robbery; yes, they have wronged and vexed the poor and needy; yes, they have oppressed the stranger and temporary resident wrongfully.

And I sought a man among them who should build up the wall and stand in the gap before me for the land, that I should not destroy it, but I found none.

Therefore, have I poured out My indignation upon them; I have consumed them with the fire of My wrath; their own way have I repaid [by bringing it] upon their own heads, says the Lord God.

If people pray, nations can be changed and saved. In *Exodus 32:7-14,* Moses interceded for the Israelites, and God changed His mind about destroying them.

II Chronicles 7:14 (AMP) states, " If My people, who are called by My name, shall humble themselves, pray, seek, crave, and require of necessity My face and turn from their wicked ways, then will I hear from heaven, forgive their sin, and heal their land."

The Bible instructs us to pray for people in authority. A lot of times, we complain about leaders and those in government, but God has called us to pray for them so our lives would be blessed. We should pray for our president, congress, and all those in positions of authority. Praying for them is our God-given responsibility. It is our Christian obligation to pray for the leaders of our nation daily. We should ask the Lord to give them the wisdom of God to deal wisely with the affairs of life. *The Book of First Timothy, Chapter 2,* begins with some very specific instructions from the Apostle Paul about praying for our leaders.

FIRST OF all, then, I admonish and urge that petitions, prayers, intercessions, and thanksgiving be offered on behalf of all men.

BE STRONG

For kings and all who are in positions of authority or high responsibility, that [outwardly] we may pass a quiet and undisturbed life [and inwardly] a peaceable one in all godliness and reverence and seriousness in every way.

__1 Timothy 2:1-2 (AMPC)

In *Numbers: Chapter 12,* Moses prayed for Miriam, who had been struck with leprosy due to talking against him. God healed her because of Moses' prayer. God instructs us many places in His Word to pray for our enemies – those who abuse and misuse us. A powerful person in prayer is the one who has been hurt by a person and is willing to lay aside their personal feelings and pray.

Job prayed for his three friends who did not minister to him in his trouble, and God gave Job twice as much as he had lost *(Job 42:10)*. I am very grateful for all the people who pray for me. Others praying for us is one of the greatest gifts that God has given to us. So continue to lift each other up in prayer, using different types of prayer.

Miranda Burnette

ABOUT THE AUTHOR

MIRANDA BURNETTE is the president and founder of Miranda Burnette Ministries, Inc. She is a licensed evangelist. She is also the founder of Keys to Success Academy, Inc., a Conference Line Leadership Bible School where she teaches people how to discover and fulfill their calling, to make their dreams a reality, to be successful in every area of their lives, and to be all God created them to be. The vision of Miranda Burnette Ministries is to educate, equip, and empower others to be successful leaders and reach their full God-given potential.

Miranda is the author of *Success Starts in Your Mind, Dare to Dream and Soar like an Eagle, Leader to Leader, Keys to Living a Fruit-Filled Life, Dare to Dream Again—*

Book and Study Guide, Winning With the Power of Love—Book and Study Guide, and Leading With Confidence—Book and Study Guide. She also makes an impact on the lives of others with her teachings on CD.

She is the founder and president of I Can Christian Academy, Inc. Miranda and her husband, Morris, lives in Atlanta, Georgia, and are the parents of two adult children, Latrelle and Davin.

CONTACT INFORMATION

For more information or to order books contact:
Miranda Burnette Ministries, Inc.
P. O. Box 314
Clarkdale, GA 30111
E-mail:
miranda@ mirandaburnetteministries.org
Website:
www.mirandaburnetteministries.org

Miranda Burnette

OTHER BOOKS BY MIRANDA BURNETTE
Dare to Dream and Soar Like an Eagle
The Sky is the Limit!

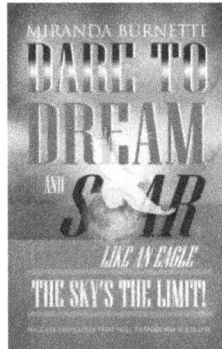

If you are ready to take the challenge to make your dreams a reality, this book is for you. In these pages, Miranda Burnette shares important success principles that will absolutely transform your life. The keys contained in this powerful book will help you soar from level to level in order to fulfill God's purpose for your life.

Dare to Dream and Soar like an Eagle will help you:

- Maximize your potential
- Achieve your goals
- Clarify your vision
- Cultivate inspired ideas
- Release the seeds of greatness that God has placed inside you
- Recognize that God created you for *SUCCESS*

It doesn't matter who you are or what you are experiencing in your life right now, you have residing within you God-given ability to accomplish more than you could ever imagine. So Dare to Dream and Soar Like an Eagle! *The Sky's the Limit!*

Success Starts In Your Mind
A Manual on How to Think Your Way to Success

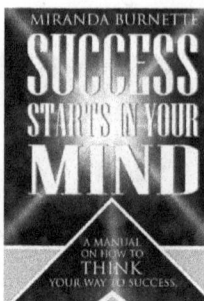

If you could change one thing in your life right now, what would you change? Have you ever considered changing your thoughts? If you are frustrated, discontented, and disappointed with your life, if you want to be successful in different areas of your life, if you want to be freed from the bondage of bad habits, and if you want your life to change, *THIS BOOK IS FOR YOU!* If you want your life to change, you have to change your thinking. Your life won't change unless your thoughts change. You can change your life by changing your thoughts.

Success Starts in Your Mind will help you:

- Understand the power of thoughts
- Develop an understanding of the relationship between success and the mind
- Think positively
- Overcome the fear of success
- Comprehend how what you think about yourself can dramatically affect your level of success
- Realize that *Success Starts In Your Mind*

If you are not successful, or if you are not as successful as you would like to be, it is time for you to start *Thinking Your Way to Success.*

Leader to Leader
Inspiring Words for Women in Leadership

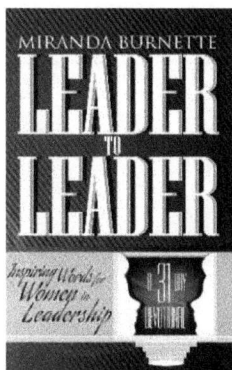

Do you want to be a strong, confident leader?

Do you want to learn leadership principles that will take you and your organization to the next level?

Do you desire to develop leaders, not just followers?

Do you want to learn how to make good decisions?

THEN THIS BOOK IS FOR YOU!

Leader to Leader will help you to:

Discover how to be an effective leader

Develop principles of leadership that will help you be the leader others will follow

Learn the qualities of a great leader

Realize that failure is not fatal

Use your past mistakes as a stepping stone to rise to the next level

Lead by example
Develop great leaders

Read, study, and meditate on the leadership principles in this devotional, and become the effective leader you've always wanted to be.

Keys to Living a Fruit-Filled Life
Nine Keys That Will Unlock the Door to Success in Your Life

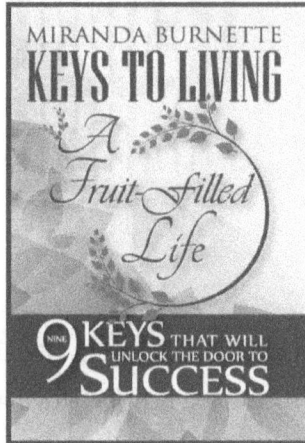

MIRANDA BURNETTE

KEYS TO LIVING

A Fruit-Filled Life

9 KEYS NINE THAT WILL UNLOCK THE DOOR TO **SUCCESS**

Do you want to have a successful, productive, fulfilling life? Would you like to have a life where you accomplish great things? Have you desired a life where you are constantly growing and over flowing with blessings and prosperity? Do you want a life that is producing good fruit? Would you like to live your life in such a way that you make a great difference in the lives of others? Do you want a life that is full of love, joy, peace, patience, kindness, goodness, humility, faithfulness, and self-control? If you answered yes to all of those questions, *THIS BOOK IS FOR YOU!*

Keys to Living a Fruit-Filled Life will teach you:

How to live a happier more peaceful life

How to prepare for great opportunities

Steps to develop the Fruit of the Spirit in your life

How to develop great relationships

Nine keys that will unlock the door to success in your life

How to live the *"Good Life"*

Keys to Living a Fruit-Filled Life will open the door to success in your life and guide you into how to enjoy the abundant life God has for you.

Dare to Dream Again
It's Never too Late For a New Beginning
Book and Study

Have you ever dreamed of winning something, being something, or starting something? Maybe you have dreamed of starting your own business, earning a degree, becoming a professional athlete, artist, or musician. We are born dreamers! When you stop dreaming, it seems as if a part of you is missing. Nothing else seems to fulfill you as much as the desire to realize or accomplish your dream.

God has a specific plan designed for each of our lives. Nevertheless, it is our responsibility to stay on the path to our dream. We must hold on to the dream, cooperate with God, and fulfill the plan He has for our lives. If you have lost sight of your dream, and given up on your dream, it is time to dream again! As you read this book, it is my sincere prayer that you will pick up the shattered pieces of your dream and rekindle the passion you once had and *Dare to Dream Again!* Once you start dreaming again, this time, don't let anyone or anything stop you from living your dream! Hold on to your dream and don't let it go!

Winning With the Power of Love
How to Love Your Way to Victory
Book and Study Guide

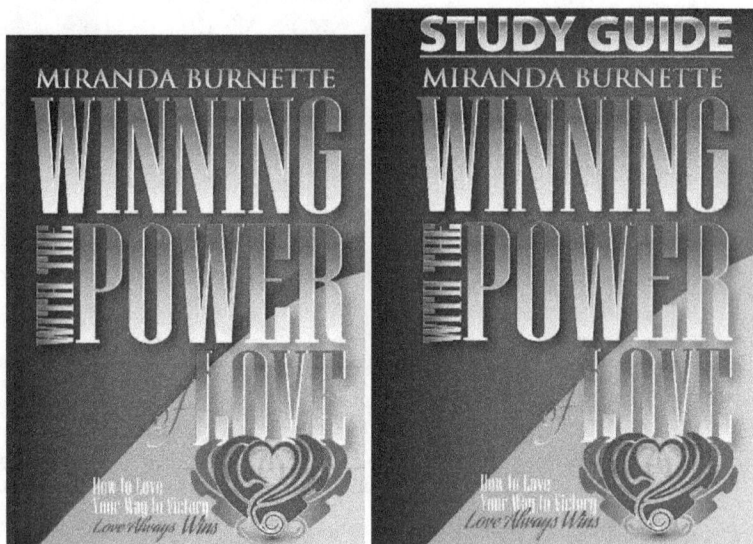

Do you want to be a winner in life? Do you want to reach your goals, be successful, have good relationships, and prosper in every area of your life? Do you want to have joy, peace, and happiness abounding in your life? Do you want to make a difference in the lives of others and help them to succeed and be winners? If your answer to all of these questions is *YES, THIS BOOK IS FOR YOU!*

Winning With the Power of Love will help you to be the winner you have always dreamed you could be. This book contains the tools you need to overcome obstacles that have been holding you back and reach your full God-given potential.

Winning With the Power of Love will teach you:
- The true meaning of being a winner
- How the power of love can literally change your life

84

- How to win with people
- How to win by loving yourself
- Why love is so powerful
- How the force of love will drive fear out of your life forever
- How walking in the power of love can increase your faith
- How many of your problems can be solved by you receiving God's love, loving yourself, loving God and loving others

If you are not loving, you are not winning. You can't lose when you love. Love has never lost a battle and it never will. You can win with the power of love. Start loving and start winning today. Building your life on the solid foundation of love will enable you to accomplish more in life than you could ever imagine.

Leading With Confidence
How to Lead and Develop Others With Confidence
Book and Study Guide

Do you want to be an effective, confident leader? Do you want to make a great impact on those whom you lead? Do you want to make things in you organization and in your life happen? Do you want to develop confident leaders? Do you want to be like a magnet that draws others to you who want to follow you? IF YES, THEN THIS BOOK IS FOR YOU!

Leading With Confidence will help you to:
- Understand the power of confidence
- Develop leadership skills in yourself and others
- Develop successful leaders
- Accomplish great things in your organization
- Be the one who others look up to
- Have a Can-Do attitude
- Grow your organization effortlessly

Start leading and developing others with confidence today!

www.ingramcontent.com/pod-product-compliance
Lightning Source LLC
Chambersburg PA
CBHW062008040426
42447CB00010B/1964